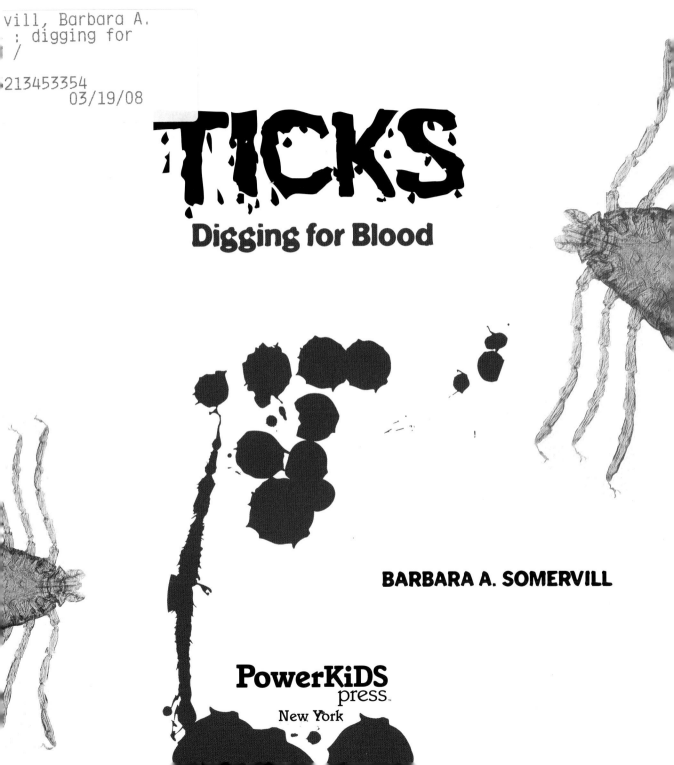

TICKS
Digging for Blood

BARBARA A. SOMERVILL

PowerKiDS press™

New York

Published in 2008 by The Rosen Publishing Group, Inc.
29 East 21st Street, New York, NY 10010

First Edition

Editors: Geeta Sobha and Joanne Randolph
Book Design: Dean Galiano
Layout Design: Greg Tucker
Photo Researcher: Nicole Pristash

Photo Credits: Cover © David Scharf/Getty Images; pp. 5, 7, 11, 15, 17 © Shutterstock.com; pp. 9, 13 by Scott Bauer, USDA Agricultural Research Service, www.forestryimages.org; p. 19 © Hans Pfletschinger/Getty Images; p. 21 by CDC/Andrew J. Brooks.

Library of Congress Cataloging-in-Publication Data

Somervill, Barbara A.
   Ticks : digging for blood / Barbara A. Somervill. — 1st ed.
      p. cm. — (Bloodsuckers)
   Includes index.
   ISBN-13: 978-1-4042-3800-8 (library binding)
   ISBN-10: 1-4042-3800-X (library binding)
   1. Ticks—Juvenile literature. I. Title.
   QL458.S63 2008
   595.4'29—dc22
                                           2006103373

Manufactured in the United States of America

CONTENTS

MEET THE TICK

Homer, the family dog, has run off into the woods again. Usually, this is okay. Today, it is not. It is July, and ticks are everywhere. As Homer runs through the bushes and weeds, ticks wait. They cannot fly or jump, they only crawl. They sit on the edges of leaves or blades of grasses.

When Homer brushes against the bushes, the ticks grab on to him. Right away, the ticks head for his ears, belly, or face. The ticks dig into the dog's skin and begin sucking blood. This is how ticks live. They drink blood to **survive**.

Ticks wait for passing animals, like this dog. As the dog brushes past, they grab on and find a place to dig in and eat.

5

SO MANY TICKS

There are two types of ticks. Soft ticks are called Argasidae (ahr-GAHS-ih-dee), and hard ticks are called Ixodidae (ik-SOD-ih-dee). Before they feed, hard ticks look like flat seeds. Their backs have a covering called the scutum (SKYOO-tuhm). The scutum is hard and shiny. Soft ticks do not have a scutum, but their skin is tough.

All ticks are bloodsuckers and feed on a wide range of animals. Ticks are classed in the same family as spiders and are closely related to mites. There are 850 different **species** of ticks.

Hard ticks feed until they are full then drop off the host to shed their skin. This tick is feeding on a person.

7

EIGHT-LEGGED BITERS

Ticks have an oval body. Mouthparts called palps are at the front of the body, and two eyes are set directly behind the mouthparts. Ticks have eight hairy legs that have hooklike claws on the ends. The claws allow ticks to hang on to their **prey**.

Some ticks are large, easily seen, and close to the size of a raisin. Others may be as small as the dot shown here: •. Ticks may be brown, red, black, or off-white in color.

This is a female black-legged tick, or deer tick. You can see the palps at the front of the oval body and the eight legs.

9

HOME IS WHERE THE HOST IS

To survive, ticks need high **humidity** and a large number of animals on which to feed. During weather with no rain, a tick's body can dry out. Ticks need 80 percent humidity to live comfortably. They hide under logs or in rotting leaves. Too much rain, though, is bad for ticks because they can die in flooded places.

The animals that ticks feed on are called hosts. Tick **larvae** feed on small rodents, birds, or reptiles. **Nymphs** go for squirrels, birds, or rabbits, while adults like cows, deer, elk, dogs, sheep, and, yes, humans.

Places that have a lot of deer often have a lot of ticks, too. Many ticks need to feed on three hosts, one for each stage of their life.

TIME TO EAT

Hard and soft ticks feed in different ways. At each stage in the **life cycle**, a hard tick will drink blood only once. The hard tick drinks for several days. That meal may carry it for up to a year or more. A hard tick may take in 200 to 600 times its unfed body weight in one feeding.

Soft ticks eat more often and eat much less. Soft ticks live in caves, animal dens, or nests. They live between the branches of a nest, for example, and suck the blood of birds there. Soft ticks like to feed on animals such as birds, bats, prairie dogs, or ferrets.

This is a female black-legged tick after eating. Its body gets larger as it fills up with blood.

QUESTING

When a tick hunts for food, it is called questing. A quest is a search, and a tick is searching for a food source. Ticks can be found where there are many animals. They are not active hunters. A tick simply waits on a branch or stem with its front legs held out. Sooner or later, an animal will brush past, picking up the tick.

The tick will grab on and find its way to the animal's skin and bite. Many ticks might fix themselves to the same host.

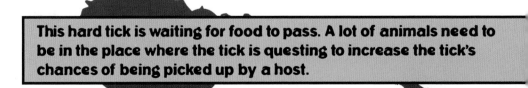

This hard tick is waiting for food to pass. A lot of animals need to be in the place where the tick is questing to increase the tick's chances of being picked up by a host.

15

TASTY TICKS

Wild chickens, grackles, cattle egrets, and oxpeckers are birds that regularly feast on ticks. Another bird, the guinea fowl, is known for eating very large amounts of ticks. Two guinea fowl can eat 2 acres (.8 ha) worth of ticks in one year.

In the insect world, a certain type of wasp, the Ichneumon (ik-NOO-mehn) wasp, lays its eggs on ticks. When the larvae come out of the eggs, they eat the ticks as they grow.

The red-billed oxpecker eats ticks, lice, fleas, and other bloodsucking insects.

17

THE LIFE OF A TICK

Some ticks live only a short time, while others have life cycles that last years. A female sheep tick lays a batch of 2,000 eggs. The larvae leave the egg ready to feed. The larvae quest for a host then feed for several days. Once full, they drop off the host. Weeks, months, or even a year passes. The larvae then shed their skin, or molt, and become nymphs.

Nymphs quest, feed, and molt. Then they become adult ticks. Adults live long enough to produce eggs and then they die.

This wood tick is laying eggs. The larvae that break out of the eggs will have six legs. Nymphs and adults have eight legs.

ILLNESSES AND TICKS

Ticks carry and spread many illnesses. The two most common in North America are Rocky Mountain spotted fever and Lyme disease.

Rocky Mountain spotted fever is uncomfortable, but it is short lived. It can cause fever, headache, aching muscles, and a rash on the wrists and ankles. Doctors use **antibiotics** to treat this illness.

Lyme disease affects about 10,000 people in the United States each year. People with Lyme disease get a fever and headaches that may last for months.

This drawing shows an American dog tick. This tick is known for spreading Rocky Mountain spotted fever.

21

CONTROLLING TICKS

Protecting yourself from ticks is important. When in forests or fields, wear light-colored clothes so you can see a tick crawling on you. Wear long pants and boots, and spray on an insect **repellent** to keep ticks away.

After being in places where ticks might be, check your body for ticks. Look under your arms, in and around your ears, behind your knees, and in your hair. Remove a tick using tweezers. To do so, grab the tick close to your skin and pull gently. Never try to squash or burn the tick out of your skin. Wash the spot with soap and water and apply an **antiseptic**.

GLOSSARY

antibiotics (an-tee-by-AH-tiks) Drugs that kill bacteria.

antiseptic (an-tee-SEP-tik) Something that is used to keep cuts clean.

humidity (hyoo-MIH-duh-tee) The amount of wetness in the air.

larvae (LAHR-vee) Animals in the early life stage in which they have a wormlike form.

life cycle (LYF SY-kul) The stages in an animal's life, from birth to death.

nymphs (NIMFS) Young insects that have not yet grown into adults.

prey (PRAY) An animal that is hunted by another animal for food.

protecting (pruh-TEKT-ing) Keeping safe.

repellent (rih-PEH-lunt) Something that keeps animals or insects away from a person or object.

species (SPEE-sheez) One kind of living thing.

survive (sur-VYV) To stay alive.

INDEX

WEB SITES

Due to the changing nature of Internet links, PowerKids Press has developed an online list of Web sites related to the subject of this book. This site is updated regularly. Please use this link to access the list:
www.powerkidslinks.com/bsu/ticks/